BILLIARDS & SNOOKER:
A Postcard Album

Roger Lee

Gentlemen wearing bowlers, boaters and cloth caps can all be seen on this turn of the century billiard room postcard.

It is hard to think of any other sport which had appeal to such a varied and broad social base. From the landed gentry in royal palaces to the unemployed in downtown billiard halls; its participants encompassed all classes of British society.

The images of after-dinner gentlemen, with their port and cigars, in fine country houses, to the 'mis-spent youth' hustling in the pool hall have been well dramatised over the years; while between, there is a truer representation of those who play these most popular of indoor games.

2. A billiard room on a real photographic postcard of around 1910 by anonymous publisher. It captures the flavour of the age, though.

GU00728976

INTRODUCTION

The Golden Ages of Picture Postcards and English Billiards partly co-incided, though that of billiards lasted longer. Postcards were at the height of their popularity from 1902-18, but suffered when the telephone and other forms of communications became widely available to the general public. Billiards' Golden Age was from 1895-1935, but declined when the likes of Walter Lindrum, Joe Davis, Tom Newman and Clarke McConachy made the game look so easy that average players could no longer identify the professionals' method of scoring with their own game.

It was not until the mid-1930's, when Joe Davis *(front cover)* popularised snooker, that it overtook billiards as the number one indoor sport.

In the time-frame of sporting history, snooker is relatively modern, being the combination of two late 19th century games. Pyramids was purely a betting game employing just 15 reds and cue ball; the first player to pot eight balls took the spoils. Life Pool, another betting game, was played with various coloured balls by any number of players who each had their own cue and object ball. By combining the reds with the coloured balls in the mid-1870's, snooker was invented.

The term 'snooker' has military origins, as it was slang for a first-year cadet with little military knowledge, who was subsequently treated with contempt by his superiors. The early exponents were British Army officers, and it is said that when one officer was left with a particularly difficult shot, he turned to his opponent and said, *"why. you're a regular snooker."*

It is impossible to place a date, even an approximate one, on the birth of billiards, but it certainly dates back to Shakespeare's days. Like most ball games, its origins are shrouded in mystery, but it seems that it began life as a form of croquet played on an indoor table, when the light or weather conditions prevented play outside.

It took at least two centuries for it to resemble anything like English Billiards we know today, viz a three-ball game of pots, cannons and in-offs, played on a 12'x6' green-baized, slate-bedded table, with six pockets and a baulk line.

Described in early 20th century literature as *"The Game Beautiful"*, billiards is a more subtle game than snooker, delightful to play, but less of a spectator sport than its more successful daughter.

On 14th November 1922, the British Broadcasting Corporation made their first wireless broadcast on 2LO. It was a news programme, was read twice, and was received only by listeners in the London area. The bulletin gave news details of a rowdy election meeting with Winston Churchill, a bank robbery, and closed with a reading of the day's billiard results. This gives some idea of the game's importance during the first quarter of this century.

Roger Lee

No Dave
Best Wishes
Roger Lee

3. A certain amount of artistic licence was allowed here with this billiard match of two million up, 2000 years ago. The stakes for 'a pot of potted shrimps' have somewhat increased over the years, too. Many variations on *Prehistoric Billiards* were published around 1905; this example was by H.J.West of Ramsgate.

LA PARTIE DE BILLARD   *Extrait de "Sports & Jeux d'adresse" de M. Henry D'Allemagne, Hachette & Cⁱᵉ*

Pt. 7   *Édition de la BELLE JARDINIÈRE_ PARIS*   *Devambez Gᵗ*

4. Louis XIV of France playing 'croquet' billiards with a mace, the forerunner to the cue, in 1694. This postcard, published by Jardiniere of Paris, is taken from an engraving by Antoine Trouvine, with the Duke of Chartres, the Count of Toulouse, and the Duke of Vendome among those attending 'La Partie De Billard.'

5. This 'Mirro-Crome' card published by H.S. Crocker Co. Inc of Baltimore is of the Raleigh Tavern Billiard Room, Williamsburg, Virginia, and illustrates an 18th century English table and early equipment.

Our Village Handicap

6. From an oil painting by Thomas Sheard (1866-1921) titled *'Our Village Handicap'*, the three characters were octogenarians who could be seen playing billiards nightly in a little village near Oxford. Card published by W.A. Belton of London in 1902.

Jolly Butchers Inn, Rawson Place.

7. The "Jolly Butchers Inn," Rawson Place, Bradford, was typical of the establishments where billiard table games of one form or another were played in the 18th and 19th centuries.

8. The "Bull & Bush Hotel" at Hampstead Heath has *Billiards and Skittles* advertised on its walls in an attempt to solicit business from passing pedestrians. Postcard published by Blum & Degen, a famous Edwardian card publisher, and posted to Plymouth in June 1907.

9. "Ye Olde Seven Stars Hotel" at Withy Grove, Manchester, had a sign outside boasting it was the oldest licensed house in Great Britain - in its 550th year then. Card published by J. Foulds of Manchester.

Ye Olde Seven Starrs Hotel, Withy Grove, Manchester
The oldest licensed house in Great Britain
The Billiard Room

10. Inside the hotel was a billiard room, where an oval table was installed at the turn of the 20th century.

6732 A   MR. F. WEISS, THE AUSTRALIAN CHAMPION.   ROTARY PHOTO. E C.
PLAYING ON THE NEW OVAL BILLIARD TABLE.

11. Despite employing the services of many of the top billiard players of the period (Australian champion Fred Weiss can be seen in action here), the oval table never caught on, and very few have survived.

Octagonal and other shapes were also tried by the table manufacturers in an attempt to create other cue games and thus boost sales. Unfortunately for the makers, billiard tables tend not to wear out - though the cloth might need replacing occasionally!

This postcard was published by the Rotary Photographic Co. Ltd of London, who specialised in personalities of the day rather than viewcards. This is no. 6732A and was posted from Stoke Newington to Cowbridge in February 1908.

Picture postcards were first published in Britain in 1894, but it was not until a decade later that they began to take off, when in 1902 the Post Office allowed a message to be written on the address side. This meant that the whole of one side was available for the picture and obviously gave more scope to publishers. All kinds of popular subjects were portrayed on postcards - Royalty, Glamour, Transport, Events - and, of course, Sport. Billiards was an appealing topic, sure to provide good sales. Edwardian postcards are now particularly sought-after by collectors, and original cards are difficult to find and can be expensive. The cards in this book are part of a collection that has taken over ten years to assemble. They cover the whole of the twentieth century, with a Stephen Hendry card the most recent.

You can find out more about postcard collecting from the magazine 'Picture Postcard Monthly', available from the publishers of this book; their address is on the back cover.

BILLIARDS AND LOVE

BILLIARDS
AND LOVE

No wonder you're
leading — I cant
play the game,
When love guides
my hand, sure,
it isn't the same!

12. *"No wonder you're leading, I can't play the game,*
  When love guides my hand, sure, it isn't the same!"
One card from a set of six published by E.A. Schwerdtfeger & Co. about 1912.

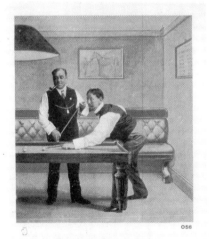

ISN'T THAT LIKE A MAN?

Chorus—

Isn't that like a man, girls?
Isn't that like a man?
When you say, "Hold the baby"; with half-hearted smile,
He says, "Can't—I'm tired"; and then, after a while,
Round a billiard table walks mile after mile—
Now, isn't that like a man?

By arrangement with Paul Mill, and Francis, Day and Hunter.

13. *"Isn't that like a man?"* was a song written by Paul Mill, published by the well-known music publishers Francis, Day and Hunter, and reproduced on a postcard. 'Song cards' like this were very popular prior to 1918.

To wish you a Merry Xmas!
and may you have
something tasty on
your
Table
this
Season!

I wish you a merry game for two,
And hope you'll get a miss.
Take my tip and use your cue,
You'll score more than a kiss.

"A Kiss off the Red."

14. A double meaning in verse with a design by Fred Spurgin from the Avenue Publishing Co. in their 'Paternoster' series.

15. Postcard published by Bamforth & Co. of Holmfirth about 1908.

Billiard Don'ts : "Don't miss a 'Kiss!'" (but kiss a Miss!)

16. *"Billiard Don'ts: 'Don't miss a kiss' but kiss a miss!"* seems good advice on this comic card drawn by Lawson Wood and one of a set of six published by Valentine of Dundee in 1907.

BILLIARD HALLS

No. 2 ROOM. *The Alexandra Billiard Rooms, 7, Victoria Street*, are the **UPSTAIRS.**
Best Ventilated and Lighted Rooms in BLACKPOOL.
8 Tables (by Burroughs & Watts). When visiting Blackpool don't forget to Visit the Alexandra.
100 up, 6d. 50 up, 3d. Pool, Pyramids, and Snooker. Also at PRESTON (10 Tables) and BURNLEY (8 Tables).

17 - 18. The first public billiard room was reputedly The Piazza in Covent Garden, London, which opened in the 1820's. At the beginning of this century, billiard halls were still few and far between, but from 1909 to 1914 a steady boom occurred. With men returning home after the First World War, the number of halls increased dramatically and, in those days, £1 per week table revenue and a ten-table room gave the proprietor a very comfortable existence. One of the largest companies involved was the Lucania Group, which had many of their clubs leased above the High Street shops of Burtons the tailors.

Hely's, Ltd.] O'HARA'S BILLIARD ROOMS, FLEET STREET. 8 First-class Tables. [*Dublin.*
These old established and well-appointed Rooms
are in every respect the most comfortable in Dublin.

19. Photographic postcard of the Imperial Billiard Hall in Bolton c. 1920.

20. Advertised as *"the largest in England"*, Gatti's Billiard Saloon in Villiers Street, London, had 30 tables when this advertising postcard was published c. 1908.

21. The Imperial Temperance Billiard Hall in Blackburn during the same era.

BILLIARD TERMS

"POT THE WHITE."

22. *'Billiard Tips'* was a set of six cards published by Millar & Lang of Glasgow. *'Pot the white'* would not be published as a postcard today, but then politieal correctness did not apply when this card was sent from Glasgow in 1910.

> Putting a billiard term with a romantic encounter was a common device used to sell postcards in the early 1900's. Artists used considerable ingenuity in drawing situations to fit a particular phrase.

23. 'A big break' was one of a set of six from James Henderson of London's *'Billiard Expressions'* series B11. This postcard was sent from Northampton in August 1916.

"A BIG BREAK."

BILLIARD EXPRESSIONS.

A KISS OFF THE CUSHION.

BILLIARD EXPRESSIONS.

PUTTING ON SIDE.

BILLIARD EXPRESSIONS.

A KISS OFF THE RED.

BILLIARD EXPRESSIONS.

A CANNON OFF THE RED.

24 - 29. A set of postcards published by Bamforth. *'Billiard Expressions'* were numbered 350-355 and published about 1913: all these cards were postally used in that year or the following one.

BILLIARD EXPRESSIONS.

POTTING THE RED.

BILLIARD EXPRESSIONS.

A GOOD BREAK.

30. The Working Men's Club and Institute Union (CIU) was formed as a limited company in 1862. It was the Reverend Solly who first devised the idea of the working men's club as a recreation centre. With over 4,000 clubs affiliated to the CIU, most of which house a billiard room, the union still organises billiards and snooker championships, which date back to 1907.

31. A fourball game of snooker, played at an unknown gentlemen's club in the 1940's. It has a sign on its wall which asks gentlemen not to get on the table, but to ask the marker (sitting 2nd from right) for the rest.

32. The Temperance Billiard Saloon, Balham, was typical of the type of hall seen in many of the country's major cities during the first half of this century. As their name implies, the chain of Temperance Billiards Halls were centres where alcoholic liquors were not supplied. They encouraged youngsters to take up the sport, and many a mis-spent youth was honed to perfection in such establishments.

This postcard scene portrays a serenity of a London long since gone. It was published by 'The Mascot' of Tooting Bec Road.

The Great Depression of the early 1930's was not bad news for the halls, but the Second World War was, and many had to close. After the war, with social and working men's clubs being allowed jackpot gaming machines, ready finance was available for them to have their own billiard rooms. With the introduction of television, the decline in billiard halls continued during the 1950's and 1960's. Ironically, colour television brought the sport back to life in the late 1960's, resulting in an upsurge of snooker clubs through the 1970's and 1980's.

TABLE DAMAGE

33. *'Billiards made easy'* was a set of six cards (series 3204) published by Davidson Bros. from designs by the famous Edwardian comic artist Tom Browne. The player should have at least one foot on the floor, but then it's *"not his own table."* This particular card was overprinted for the Christmas market.

34. The famous push, screw back and tear the cloth shot! One to make any table owner sweat. Postcard from a set published by Millar & Lang in their 'National' series.

SEASIDE DIGS

35. Nothing like a good firm bed to lie on, though here in Margate the only apparent choice was a billiard table. This theme was used in many variations, and with different resorts overprinted. The message on this particular card sent from Margate on 4th September 1914 (a month after World War One broke out) reads: *"Dear Miss Thompson, Thanks very much for card, do hope you are having as good a time as I am. I haven't a boy for regulars, but a different one each day. I am leading quite a flirt's life. Much love, BC."* Card produced by the Regent Publishing Co.

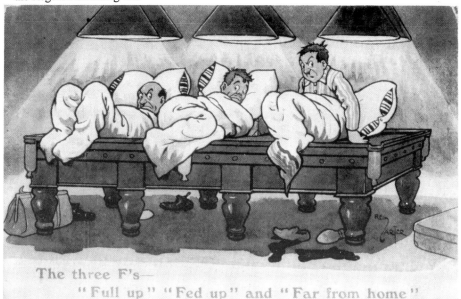

36. This card, published by Salmon of Sevenoaks from a Reg Carter comic design, was obviously intended for those who were not having a happy holiday!

MANUFACTURERS

37. Willie Holt was a billiard professional, a table manufacturer, and owner of several billiard halls in the north-west of England. He was also something of a philosopher, as the message on the wall outside his billiard hall near Stoke reads: *"To father! You need a change of thought...To Son! You need to know human nature...Billiards can help you both!"* Well, if it brought in the punters, why not?

38. Willie Holt stands outside his shopfront at his billiard table works in Burnley, on an advertising postcard for Bonzoline billiard balls. This brand name for early composition balls - as opposed to ivory - was certainly good news for elephants. At one time, it was estimated that the manufacture of billiard balls in Britain alone involved the annual slaughter of 12,000 elephants. The number of balls cut from a tusk averaged five, and the best ivory came from elephants from Equatorial Africa. Postcard sent from Burnley in August 1908.

39. J.Ascott & Co. were billiard table makers from Stratford. Established in 1850, they were wholesale and export manufacturers to the trade. Many of these smaller companies either closed or were taken over by larger concerns when the sport suffered a downturn in the late 1940's and early 1950's.

W. D. STEVENS & CO., BILLIARD TABLE MAKERS, &c., 33 BALHAM HILL, LONDON, S.W.

40. W.D. Stevens & Co. of 33 Balham Hill, London SW, were another table manufacturing company. Here three of their table fitters are, from left to right, testing the level of the bed with a spirit level; re-covering a cushion rail; and fitting a pocket and side rail to the table. These were true craftsmen, who served long apprenticeships to acquire the necessary skills to erect a true-running billiard table.

41. Burroughes & Watts were leading table manufacturers: formed in 1836, they had offices and showrooms at 19, Soho Square, London. At the end of the last century, they added their 150-seater matchroom, which was to play host to all the leading amateur and professional players until its closure in 1966. This card advertises a facsimile of the table on which John Roberts Jun. played Edward Diggle at Henglers in 1906.

42. A superb advertising postcard for E.J. Riley Ltd, Billiard Table Builders of Accrington, illustrating (from left to right): *"a billiard & dining table as a billiard table from £13.10s; a portable billiard table top to place on your dining table from £3 each; and the same table as a dining table."* Great detail and artwork on this card, but the town name is unfortunately spelled incorrectly.

A Group of Billiard Table Makers.

43. This card, published locally by Overend, illustrates the workforce at Riley's of Accrington in 1904. In the 1890's, Mr E.J. Riley, the founder of the business, joined forces with a Mr Kenyon, and together they formed a limited company, which also produced bowls equipment and cricket bats. They opened their first billiard hall in 1910, and at that time their factory in Accrington was producing 800 tables a year. Riley's today operates the largest chain of snooker clubs in the UK, and holds the current contract for all televised professional tournaments.

After Joe Davis's retirement from the World Professional Snooker Championships in 1946, he became a director of Leicester Square Hall, where he made the first official 147 break against his old adversary, Willie Smith. At this venue and others, Joe raised large sums of money for various charities, and in 1968 was awarded the OBE.

It warms the heart today to think Joe saw some of the benefits of his labours. This must have been evident to him during the 1978 Embassy World Snooker Championship, while watching his younger brother Fred playing his semi-final match. As Joe took his seat at the 'Crucible' in Sheffield, the packed audience rose as one to applaud him. Sadly, before the final, Joe was taken ill, and the man who for one whole generation embodied everything good about the game, died a few months later (see illustrations 1, 108, and 109)

44. HRH The Prince of Wales, later Edward VIII of abdication fame, looks almost interested as he tours a table factory in the late 1920's; this particular firm made miniature tables.

Royalty as spectators date back at least to the days when Edward VII, then Prince of Wales, attended the first professional tournament between John Roberts Sen. and William Cook at St. James's Hall, London, in 1870.

Mary, Queen of Scots, was an avid player, and complained bitterly when she was deprived of her table while a state prisoner at Fotheringay Castle in 1576.

In 1605, James I asked for a 'billiarde bourde' to be constructed; but the game took a serious setback during George II's reign, when he ordered the playing of billiards to be banned in public places.

King George IV and Queen Caroline both enjoyed the game, and Queen Victoria also had tables supplied.

Charles Dawson and Harry Stevenson (see illustrations 94 and 95) played each other four times for the Professional Billiards Championship early this century. Their last encounter was at the National Sporting Club, and as in previous matches, a great deal of negotiating preceded it. The one point they did agree upon was to play on a table made by Rileys, a 'northern' company. This decision did not go down too well with the establishment, the Billiards Association, who had members from other firms on its committee.

By 1908, Dawson's eyesight was failing, and he soon had to retire. Like so many players of that era, he died in penury, in 1921.

Harry Stevenson, however, went from strength to strength, became champion in 1909, and successfully defended his title against Melbourne Inman on three further occasions.

Like most sporting activities, the championship was suspended during the First World War, and on its resumption in 1919, Stevenson lost in the final to Inman.

He died in 1944.

45. This less than reverent comic French postcard titled *'Une partie de carambolage,'* illustrates monks playing the continental carom game, which has no table pockets, and scoring by cannon play only. Card sent from Paris in 1904.

46. The monks' common room at Douai Abbey, Woolhampton, Berkshire, housed a three-quarter size table with six legs. This postcard was postally used in 1918.

47. Billiards was considered by certain religious and public schools as good recreation for their pupils. Their 'education' was carried on at many of the major universities, and Oxford and Cambridge used to have their own varsity matches. The first National Boys' under-16 Championship was staged in 1922 and won by Walter Donaldson, who in 1947 also won the World Professional Snooker Championship. This postcard of the billiard room at St. Augustine's Abbey School was published by Carr & Son, Ramsgate photographers.

An amusing incident concerning top billiard player Walter Lindrum (see illustrations 110-113) occurred when one of his opponents visited the hall well before the start of a match, and was asked if he'd come to examine the table. "No," came the reply, "I've come to select a comfortable chair!"

Although he could make century breaks at snooker, Walter never entered the World Championships; if he had, maybe the record books would read differently. The comparison with Jimmy White in style has often been remarked upon.

Walter made yearly visits to the British Isles from 1929 to 1933, but because of contractual table restrictions (yet again), only entered the World Professional Billiards Championships twice, and was successful on each occasion against Joe Davis.

The rest of his career was spent, for the most part, playing exhibition matches world-wide, in which he raised large sums of money for worthwhile causes. He was awarded the OBE in 1958, just two years before his untimely death.

LEAGUE TEAMS

All sports need their grass roots for future champions to develop. As billiards, and then snooker, increased in popularity, so the local leagues grew. Shown here are two postcards of winning teams from their respective localities.

Fartown and Birkby Liberal Club, Ltd.   Billiard Team, 1913-14.
Winners of the Huddersfield and District Liberal Clubs' Billiard Cup.

48. Fartown and Birkby Liberal Club were winners of the Huddersfield and District Billiards Cup in season 1913-14, the photographic evidence preserved by this card from W.E. Turton of Huddersfield.

49. The winning team in the Grimsby League during the late 1950's.

HOTELS

Hotels have often used the billiard room as a facility to attract customers, and here are two good examples.

50. The Highfield Hotel of unknown location had a proprietor named L.H. Ship, and housed a fine Burroughes & Watts table.

THE BILLIARD ROOM, STRAND PALACE HOTEL.

51. The Strand Palace in London, with three tables, was well-publicised by this postcard from W.H. Smith in the 'Kingsway Real Photo' series.

CLUBS AND HOMES

52. Members of all political parties of every colour, whether 'potting reds on the bed' or 'cueing down the blues' have often utilised the club's billiard room as a smoke-filled area of policy-making. Conversely, local inhabitants have often become members to use the facilities, even if they have been of the opposite political persuasion! It also gets used as a changing room for visiting cabaret artistes! The Conservative Club at Beccles is one such typical room.

53. Billiards and snooker are ideal pastimes for a patient's recovery, and here the Transport and General Workers Union Convalescent Home at Littleport was well-supported, as seen here on this postcard published by *The Daily Herald.*

MILITARY CUES

6   BILLIARD ROOM, PRIVATES' RECREATION ROOM, PORTSMOUTH DIVISION. R.M.L.I.   PHOTO.
GALE & POLDEN. LTD.

54. Many a young serviceman's introduction to the billiard table has been in the regiment's club room. Interestingly, the naval players above are playing a game of skittles on the billiard table, which is a most skilful and sometimes a most frustrating game, seen very little these days. Players had to avoid knocking down the skittles while playing a conventional game of billiards. This real photograph was by Gale & Polden Ltd of Nelson House, Portsmouth.

> *Mark Twain, billiards fan (see illustration 90), once told this tale about the game: "Once, when I was an underpaid reporter in Virginia City, a stranger came to town and opened a billiard parlour. I went to see him and he proposed a game, to which I agreed. 'Before we can begin,' he said, 'knock the balls around a little so I can assess if any handicapping is required.' I did so for a while and then he said, 'I'll be perfectly fair with you: I'll play you left-handed.' I felt hurt at this, for he was cross-eyed, freckled and had red hair, so I was determined to teach him a lesson for his audacity. But he won the toss, got in straight away, and continued to play the game out, after which he took my half-dollar, and all I got was the opportunity to chalk my cue. 'If you play like that with your left hand,' I said, 'I'd like to see you play with your right.' 'I can't,' was the prompt reply. 'I'm left-handed.' "*

55. The billiard room at the Trafalgar Institute, Portsmouth, illustrates another example of naval cuemanship, but the sailor looks a novice, as he could have played the shot without the rest!

56. First World War action from the billiard room at Forton Barracks. The sender writes that he is about to be demobbed; the card was posted from Gosport in 1919.

57. Here the 1st Royal Regiment, of the British Silesian Forces in 1922, are enjoying a game on a halfsize table.

58. These are makeshift tables, so true running of the balls looks suspect. That was probably the last thing on the mind of the sender of this postcard, as he was writing to his sweetheart, saying he was just going out on a night attack from Hedon, Yorks.

59. Compliments of the season on this advertising card from Hobson & Son, Military Outfitters, of Lexington Street, Golden Square, London. It was posted in 1904. The painter was the incomparable military artist Harry Payne, famous for his long and accurate series of regimental postcards.

60. Off-duty relaxation here for the Kings Rifle Corps, but should dogs be allowed in the games room? This postcard was published by Gale & Polden Ltd.

THE KING'S ROYAL RIFLE CORPS.
Off Duty.

61. A view of the billiard room, Sandringham House, photographed by F. Ralph of Dersingham and Hunstanton, Norfolk. The Prince of Wales tulip insignia is carved on the table legs.

62. This card, posted at Bakewell in 1912, is of Chatsworth House. The table is of a much older design, being of lightweight construction, and probably made by Gillow & Co.

16 OSBORNE-HOUSE (Isle of Wight). — Billiard Room. — LL.

63. The most common postcards relating to Royal Palaces are those of Queen Victoria's Osborne House on the Isle of Wight, showing the table and decorations designed by Prince Albert. This example is no. 16 in a series published by Lucien Levy of Paris.

The first table to be installed at Buckingham Palace was in 1836. This was later replaced by a table from Thurstons, the game's oldest table manufacturers, who had several royal patrons. They supplied Queen Victoria with the first set of rubberised cushions, which replaced stuffed felt in the 1840's, for a table at Windsor Castle.

From the early 1920's many of the game's leading exponents, including Walter Lindrum, Tom Reece, Melbourne Inman, and the one-armed player and referee, Arthur Goundrill, gave Royal Command Exhibitions at Buckingham Palace. A nice quote attributed to Edward VII was *"no 'gentleman' ever made a break of more than 25."*

COUNTRY HOUSES

64. The country house was a natural home for a billiard room, with its high ceilings and spacious dimensions. The minimum size for a full-size table is 22 x 16 ft, which does not allow for seating. For the 'after dinner set', much more room would be required, and the above example - location unknown - was ideal.

65. Another beautifully-furnished billiard room. This is Llanhydrock House in Cornwall, which is owned by the National Trust.

66. This gentleman, caricatured by Dudley Buxton, having 'a ripping time,' would not have been out of place in any of these country houses.

HOLIDAY CAMPS

BUTLIN'S MINEHEAD
The Billiard Room

67. Over the past fifty years, many youngsters would have seen their first full-size snooker table at a holiday camp, where father 'taught' them the rules and how to hold a cue. If they were very lucky, they could get coaching from a world champion, such as John Pulman, seen above at Butlin's, Minehead, in 1968.

BUTLIN'S FILEY—*A Billiard Room*   *Photo: E. Nägele, John Hinde Studios*

68. By the positioning of the balls, it looks as if the photographer, E. Nagele of Hinde Studios, Dublin, had a hand in their distribution. The card features Butlin's at Filey in 1969.

INSTRUCTIONAL

69. Cannon, screws and pocketing are all demonstrated here by Alec Taylor, the *"well-known expert,"* on this Rotary Photo card no. 3983D.

70. This delightful lady, photographed by Carlton of Horncastle, is all dressed up with nowhere to go! Ladies in billiard table fancy dress followed a popular theme during the first quarter of this century. There was also the ladies' argument, *"he's always on the billiard table, so if you can't beat them, be one!"*

71. Another fancily-dressed lady who obviously finds it cooler in the shade!

72. Like many sports over the years, billiards and snooker have been a male preserve, with the fairer sex often being banned from the billiard room. This has caused problems, particularly with visiting teams with lady players, and in some extreme cases, actions have gone to court. Fortunately, in these more liberated days, such cases are few and far between. As this postcard shows, this was not a problem with this mixed foursomes of the 1920's, and, to judge by the lady cueing, she was a very useful player.

73. There is no obvious physical reason why ladies cannot play to the same standard as men. In the 1930's and 1940's, the top three lady players were Joyce Gardner, Ruth Harrison, and our subject, Thelma Carpenter, photographed here in the early 1930's by Cummings of Weymouth.

Although below the standard of their male counterparts, they did have their own tournaments, and in club exhibitions were capable of beating any male members, which always created a good evening's entertainment.

THE AMATEURS

MR HARRY C. VIRR
AMATEUR BILLIARD CHAMPION
1907 — 8 — 11.

74. The Amateur Billiards Championships were inaugurated in 1888, and Harry Virr won the title six times between 1907 and 1914. He then retired and was allowed to keep the large trophy illustrated, which went on view at the Northgate Hotel, Bradford, which was run by the Virr family for many years. The location of the trophy today is unknown.

75. Joe Thompson was amateur billiard champion in 1936, and is seen here with the larger John Roberts Trophy. This was originally the professional's trophy from 1870, but with Roberts winning the championship on so many occasions, he was eventually presented with it, and it remained in the family until 1930. His son then left it in trust to the amateur body, and it is still played for to this day.

SAUCY GAME

"Here's a joke! My husband has just rung up to say, that he's playing billiards with you!!"

"YOU MUSN'T TOUCH ME, I'M IN BAULK!"

76. This 'New Donald McGill' comic (no. 1006) was posted from Blackpool (where else?) in 1942.

77. From the Philco Publishing Co. - series no. 5520, issued about 1908.

"THERE'S ONLY THE **BRIDAL SUITE** LEFT, SIR!"
"BUT WE'VE BEEN MARRIED FOR TWENTY FIVE YEARS"
"SO WHAT— IF I PUT YOU IN THE BILLIARD ROOM, YOU NEEDN'T PLAY RUDDY BILLIARDS ALL NIGHT!!"

78. 1970's comic postcard, drawn by Fitzpatrick and published by Bamforth & Co in 'Comic' series no. 581.

THURSTON'S

Passed by Censor.   THURSTON'S, Leicester Square.

79. A soldier rummages amongst the debris of Thurston's Matchroom, Leicester Square, after a German bomb blitzed it in 1940. He is picking up scoreboard nameplates of famous players who graced this venue from 1901.

The table survived, but many of the game's treasures were lost, as a great deal of the sport's memorabilia was on exhibition at the time - in London...during a war?

Thurston's name is synonymous with billiards and snooker, as it was John Thurston in 1814 who became the first specialised manufacturer of billiard tables, and who later brought many improvements to it, for example the slate bed and rubber cushions.

The site was redeveloped in 1947 under different management, and although renamed The Leicester Square Hall, it remained 'Thurston's' to many.

This postcard has been 'passed by the censor,' as was required during the Second World War.

PAW SHOTS

80. *'A game of billiards'* was published about 1907 by C.W. Faulkner & Co. in 'London' series no. 1165.

81. *'Billiards'* by the famous cat artist Louis Wain (1860-1939) was published recently on a modern card by Chris Beetles Ltd.

TAKE YOUR NOSE OFF THE TABLE—
YOUR'E ONLY ALLOWED TO PLAY WITH
ONE RED!

POTTING THE RED!

82. Card published in the early 1920's by Wildt & Kray of London. Drunken-ness was a popular theme with comic postcard artists.

83. Cartoon by Reg Maurice, issued by the Regent Publishing Co. about 1925 (card no. 4442).

"CANNON OFF THE RED"

84. Billiard terms lent themselves admirably to double meaning illustrations. Another card from Millar & Lang.

KEEP SHTILL, SAM! HOW CAN I SHOP THE BALL
WITH YOU HICCOUGHING LIKE THAT?

85. Drawn by Douglas Tempest, this is
no. 23 in the 'Comic' series published by
Bamforth.

ONLY MANAGED 30 TO-DAY,
HOPE TO KNOCK OFF MORE
TO-MORROW.

86. Card no. 5076 from the Regent Publishing Co., and designed by Reg Maurice.

"FOLLOWING IN FATHER'S FOOTSTEPS."

"I think Billiards would be my game if the table & cues were a bit smaller."

87. *"Following in father's footsteps"* was designed by Crackerjack and appeared on Davidson Bros.' series 7000 as card no. 1 in a set of six.

88. A Fred Buchanan design published by Woolstone Bros. in the 'Jester' series.

With Alcock & C°'s compliments 1905

89. A charming postcard of 1905, showing aborigine children playing in the outback on a makeshift table. This card was produced for Australian table manufacturers Alcock & Co.

FAMOUS NAMES

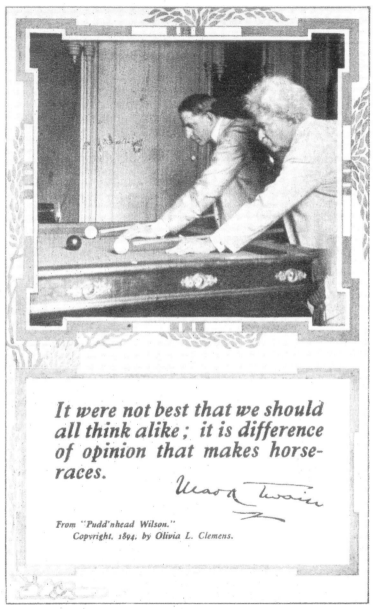

It were not best that we should all think alike; it is difference of opinion that makes horse-races.

Mark Twain

From "Pudd'nhead Wilson."
Copyright, 1894, by Olivia L. Clemens.

90. Both games over the years have had their fair share of musical and literary supporters: Mozart, Charles Dickens, Arthur Conan Doyle, J.B. Priestly - and Mark Twain, as this postcard illustrates.

91. Another fanciful theory on the origin of billiards is that in the 16th century William Kew, a pawnbroker, was in the habit during wet weather of taking down the three balls from his sign and pushing them around his counter and into his stalls with a yardstick. This became a great amusement for the clergymen from nearby St. Paul's, hence the name can(n)on. The game became known as billyard *'because William (Bill) did first play with yard measure.'* 'Cue' came from his surname. This particular card was drawn by W. Stocker Shaw and posted at Maidstone in August 1918.

92. Clever use of the word 'billiards' in this Tempest-designed comic from Bamforth ('Comic' series no. 2242), and another good reason never to install sash windows! Several variations on this joke appeared on various postcards. This one was sent from Sharnbrook, Bedfordshire, in August 1927.

THE MASTERS

93. John Roberts Jun. was the 'King of English Billiards' from 1875 to the early 1900's, and stands out as one of the great Victorians in the world of sport. He was to billiards what W.G. Grace was to cricket and was easily the most commanding figure the game has ever known, both on and off the table.

He played in front of royalty many times and did countless world tours, including India, where the Maharajah of Jaipur made him, for one month's play a year, a court billiards player for life, on an annual salary of £500 with expenses.

Roberts was a showman, immaculately dressed, a legacy he has passed down to today's players. The other side of the coin, however, was to behave as if he was a law unto himself in everything connected with billiards. The governing body and other professionals were waved aside by a sweep of his dictatorial hand.

He won the professional championship on eight occasions, the last in 1885.

This card was published by Scott Russell & Co of Birmingham and Sheffield, in the 'Scott' series of bromide photos.

MR. JOHN ROBERTS

94. Charles Dawson and Harry (H.W) Stevenson were rivals around the turn of this century; in fact they hated each other. Between 1900 and 1903, they played each other four times for the Professional Billiards Championship, Dawson winning on three occasions.

This view card of the match between Dawson and Stevenson at Newcastle-Upon-Tyne records that Stevenson made a break of 788 in 47 minutes.

95. Following in John Roberts' footsteps, Stevenson secured a lucrative South African and Indian tour in 1911 with George Gray, and they are seen here at an army officers' mess in Bloemfontein.

96. George Gray, the Australian 'boy wonder,' came to this country in the second decade of this century and proceeded to amass phenomenal breaks, mostly by playing the in-off shot into the centre pocket with monotonous regularity. By gauging the strength and direction of the shot so well, he could make the red travel up the table and back off the top cushion to within an inch of its previous position. From this scoring method, he could make a thousand break almost at will. His top break was one of 2196.

97-98. George Gray was contracted by E.J. Riley to tour and play on their tables, and these two view cards of matches record the feats Gray was achieving. These amazing breaks were made with composition balls, but in the professional championship, ivories were still being employed, which Gray never came to terms with. Because of this he never won the title, and with the advent of the First World War returned to Australia.

99. This postcard shows Tom Reece playing the famous anchor cannon stroke which he made famous in 1907.

For over five weeks he had the two object balls suspended on either jaw of the top pocket, and continued to score cannon after cannon until he had amassed a score of 499,135 points unfinished. His hapless opponent was Joe Chapman (centre), who had to get dressed each day, and sit and watch, which was just a little easier than being the poor referee. Reece had a cruel sense of humour, and would turn to his opponent and ask, *"what chalk are you using?"* or, *"how are you finding the table?"* Because of this monster break, the anchor cannon was subsequently barred.

This postcard was published in the Rotary Photographic Series No 2472 A.

Around 1905, top billiards exponent John Roberts (see illustration 93) was still a force to be reckoned with, although time was beginning to take its effect. The story goes that Charles Dawson was playing him after receiving a considerable start, when one of Roberts' supporters asked the referee who he thought would win. The referee replied that the thought Dawson would. "Well, he can't," replied the supporter, "nobody will ever beat Roberts". The referee then suggested that Roberts was not so young as he used to be and that Anno Domini might beat him. "Oh," said Roberts' backer, "I didn't mean by any of your foreign players, I meant by an Englishman!" Needless to say, Anno Domini did finally beat Roberts, who died in his 72nd year on December 23rd 1919.

100. This Burroughes & Watts advertising postcard, printed by Hill, Siffhen & Co of Holloway, gives another view of the anchor stroke Reece used in his record break. It also reads that the red ball was found to revolve vertically once in 250 strokes, whilst the opponent's white ball completed its horizontal revolutions once in 800 strokes. The condition of the referee was not noted!

"ANCHORED."

101. Perhaps this is how the referee finished up! The design was by an artist who identified himself only by his initials.

7173 A   M. INMAN   ROTARY PHOTO. E.C.

102. Affectionately known as the 'Twickenham Terrier,' Melbourne Inman was a great stroke player, a real battler, who had the ability of irritating his opponent, none more so than the more temperamental Tom Reece. There was great rivalry between them, and in one match, Inman was fluking in a manner which made Reece's hair stand on end. Taking as much as he could, Reece finally jumped up and asked with solemnity and disbelief: *"how did you get that shot, Mr Inman?"* After a momentary pause Inman replied, *"I believe you know my terms for tuition, Mr Reece".*

    From 1908 to 1919, Inman won the professional championship of billiards on five occasions, beating Tom Reece in three matches before the First World War intervened.

    The immaculately-dressed Melbourne Inman is seen here on this Rotary Photograph no. 7173 .

103. Melbourne Inman travelled to Saskatoon in November 1914 to play Willie Hoppe (1887-1959), the great American carom champion. Over the years, attempts have been made to play meaningful exhibitions, with different disciplines, on different size tables. But what usually happened was that the champion of his chosen game completely outplayed the other, and this 'Championship Billiard Exhibition' of 1914 was no exception.

The photographer was J.P. Anderson of Saskatoon.

104. Willie Smith and Tom Newman crossing cues before a match at Burroughes & Watts' salon in Soho Square, London, in May 1913. Admission prices for spectators were five shillings, three shillings, and one shilling and sixpence.

105. Willie Smith, formerly a linotype operator from Darlington, only entered the Billiard Championship twice, and won it on both occasions. The first was in 1920, against that wonderful touch player Claude Falkiner, and then in 1923 he regained the title from Tom Newman. Willie was possibly the best non-specialised, all round billiard player of all time. He played the game the average club player could identify with, making shots they would attempt. The only difference was that Willie usually got them.

As this personally autographed postcard reads, his best break was one of 2743, which must have taken great strength and concentration, as there were no quick repetitive close cannon shots in Willie's game.

His reasons for not entering the championship more often were due to his constant wrangles with the governing body, a phenomenon which is still repeated in many sports today.

Like many of the old-time billiard professionals, Willie never really took to snooker, but almost reluctantly played the 22 ball game to earn a living. When asked in 1980 if he enjoyed watching the World Snooker Championships on television, he replied he would have enjoyed it a lot more if they changed the rules. *"Which rules?"* he was asked. *"All of them,"* he replied.

106. Tom Newman was cast in a completely different mould to his more boisterous contemporary Willie Smith. Thought by most to be a cockney, Tom was actually born at Barton on Humber in Lincolnshire, and his real name was Tom Pratt; not hard to understand the change. Tom was such a gracious person, it was impossible after a match to tell whether he had won or lost, such was his amiable nature. There was never a bad word spoken of Tom Newman.

His first century break at the three ball game came when he was just 11 years of age, and in 1919 he held the official record snooker break of 89. His billiard break of 1370 in 1924 will stand forever, as it was made with ivory balls, which were replaced by composition balls in all tournaments from 1927.

This was the year Tom entered the first World Snooker Championship, losing to Melbourne Inman. Tom did make the final with Joe Davis in 1934; they had to - they were the only contestants!

Tom writes on the back of this postcard that he hopes the cartoon will please the recipient.

107. Tom won his first world professional billiard title in 1921, and his last was in 1927. This postcard shows him receiving the trophy in 1922, when his opponent was Claude Falkiner.

This postcard was published by Barratts Photo Press Ltd, 89 Fleet St, London EC4.

SEAMAN'S, PHOTOGRAPHER, CHESTERFIELD

108. Joe Davis was born on April 15th 1901 in the coal mining village of Whitwell, Derbyshire, and was Chesterfield billiards champion by the time he was 13. Early reports of his professional career gave a clear indication of his potential, and the success which was to follow.

There were new, quite distinctive features in Joe's cue action, which held him in good stead when he later turned his attention to snooker. For example, his method of sighting right down over the cue, and his ultra rigid stance, were both considered worthy of note in the billiard press of 1923. Tom Newman remarked some years later, when Joe was getting the better of him in the billiard championships, that it was Joe's potting which made the difference, resulting in as much as 3000 points advantage over a fortnight's play.

He won the professional billiards championship for the first time in 1928, after which the whole of Chesterfield, it appeared, turned up at the railway station to welcome him home.

109. Joe Davis and Clark McConachy 'stringing' for a break at a club exhibition in Bournemouth.

A Souvenir
of my Australian tour in
aid of the Red Cross and
Comforts Fund, sponsored
by the distributors of
Black & White Cigarettes.

Walter Lindrum

1942

110. Walter Lindrum (1898-1960) was simply a genius at the three-ball game of English billiards. Born in Kalgoolie, Western Australia, no champion of any sport overshadowed his contempories to the same extent. So superior was Walter in every department of the game, that by 1930, he was giving Joe Davis, Tom Newman and Clark McConachy 7000 point starts in a fortnight's play. During one of his breaks, he could occupy the table for three or four hours at a time, and would never look like missing. He conquered his chosen sport perhaps more thoroughly than any other sportsman has ever done, and his record break of 4137 remains unchallenged to this day. Incredibly, immediately after Walter's break, Joe Davis replied with a 1247, which in many ways, he considered his finest, bearing in mind what he had to follow!

On one occasion, a country lad 'came up to town' and wandered into Thurston's matchroom. After watching Lindrum for some considerable time, he turned to the doorman and asked, *"What is the game he is playing?"* *"Billiards, sir"*, came the reply. *"Oh"*, said the lad, *"they play billiards with two players where I came from, but I suppose it's different in London".*

This was symptomatic of billiards' eventual decline, for unlike snooker, billiard breaks could be stereotyped, and no matter what new restrictions the game's governing body placed on the leading exponents, these made little difference to the likes of Walter Lindrum.

111-112. Not unlike today's top players, Walter was not averse to supplementing his income away from the table. Here he is putting his signature and endorsing pens by Watermans; he also advertised Thomas Padmore & Son's billiard tables, which were manufactured in Birmingham.

W. LINDRUM (IN PLAY) V. T. A. DENNIS.

WHEN AT SKEGNESS JOE DAVIS. WILLIE SMITH. CLARK MCCONACHY AND CLAUDE FAULKNER.
ALL PLAY AT THE T. A. DENNIS BILLIARD LOUNGE, 45, HIGH STREET. SKEGNESS OPP CO-STORES
BEST TABLES IN TOWN.

113. Billiard room proprietors would also use Walter's name in promoting their premises on postcards, and here he is seen at Tom Dennis's Billiard Lounge at 45, High Street, Skegness.

T. A. DENNIS. NOTTS CHAMPION SINCE 1904.
BILLIARD PROFESSIONALS' ASSOCIATION CHAMPION
LONDON 1913 · 14 ·

Billiard Professionals' Association Champion, 1928.
Finalist English Snooker Championship, 1927.
At Thurston's, June 2nd, 1923. Dennis made 76 break in
B.P.A. Snooker Championship Final— World's Record for Snooker Final.

114-115. Tom Dennis was a Nottingham billiards professional, but is best remembered for being Joe Davis's opponent in the final of the first World Snooker Championship in 1927. His claim here, a year later, was that he made at Thurston's on 23rd June 1923 a break of 76, which was a record for a snooker final. How times have changed! Photo by Spencer Higson of Nottingham.

116. Horace Lindrum (1912-74) was Walter's nephew, and became Australian professional snooker champion by the age of 19. He first came to Britain in 1936, and in that year reached the final of the World Snooker Championships, but lost to Joe Davis by 34 frames to 27.

He lived in England throughout the 1930's - one of his addresses is shown on this postcard - but returned to Australia during the Second World War. Horace came back to England in 1946, and contested one of the great snooker finals at the Royal Horticultural Hall in London. Played over a fortnight's duration, each session was packed out with a thousand spectators. Horace lost again to Joe Davis 78-67 in the best of 155 frames.

HORACE LINDRUM
(Australian Billiard and Snooker Champion)

51, LANGDON PARK ROAD

HIGHGATE

N 6

Telephone: MOUntview 3403

117. Though he didn't have the big match temperament of Joe Davis, Horace was certainly one of the all-time great exhibition players. With his pleasing personality, he was very popular, and eagerly sought-after to demonstrate his expertise. He could perform amazing finger spins with the billiard balls, and his trick shots were spectacular. He is seen here cueing at one such event.

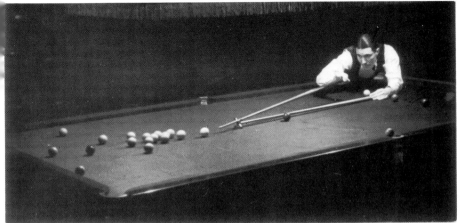

118. Sydney Smith, a contemporary and friend of Horace Lindrum, is best remembered as the first player to make an official clearance - 133 - at snooker, achieving this in 1936. The same evening, King Edward VIII was making his abdication speech. Sydney also entered the World Snooker Championships in 1936, and lost by the odd frame (15-16) to his namesake and billiard sparring partner Willie Smith. He made it to the semi-finals the following year, and in both 1938 and 1939 went one better, getting to the finals, where he met Joe Davis, losing 37-24 and 43-30. Like so many promising careers, Sydney's was interrupted by the war, after which, along with Joe Davis, he became a director of the newly-opened Leicester Square Hall.

When it closed in 1955, and snooker declined in popularity, Sydney broke off all connections with the sport, and never renewed them, even during the revival of the late 1960's.

FOR AN

Entertainment on a Billiard Table

WRITE FOR TERMS AND DATES TO

ARTHUR L. GOUNDRILL

(ONE-HAND CHAMPION & ROYAL ENTERTAINER)

75, CHURCH ROAD, RICHMOND,
SURREY.

Telephone   -   -   Richmond 0360

119. Arthur Goundrill was affectionately nicknamed 'Goundrill the Scoundrel' by his contemporaries. Despite losing his left fore-arm at Ypres during the First World War, he still became an accomplished player, a formidable trick-shot artist, and one of the sport's most respected referees. In the 1930's, when players like Lindrum and Davis were making such large breaks at rapid speed, the concentration required by the referee was enormous, for apart from recording the break, he had to remember how many shots of one particular method had been played, and inform the player accordingly. He would often have to offici-ate for eight hours a day for a fortnight, as he did in the World Billiards final at the Dor-land Hall, London, in 1933. In this match between Lindrum and Davis, 77,968 points were scored, and Goundrill called them all.

MODERN CARDS

There was an upsurge in the late 1980's in postcard publishing, and today's 'moderns' will become very collectable in a few year's time. The following two postcards were both in the *'Matchroom Players'*, series one, advertising the Official Matchroom Fan Club.

120. When it comes to snooker in the 1980's, one name - Steve Davis - stands out way above the rest. He won the Embassy World Professional Championship on six occasions between 1981 and 1989.

121. Jimmy White, who should have won that title on at least three occasions, is unfortunately remembered as the best player who has never won it - yet.